The
Christmas
Search

The Christmas Search

by Susie Whiting

ISBN: 1-55517-532-5

Published by Whiting Family Publishing

Typeset by Virginia Reeder
Cover Art by Brian Wingett

Printed in the United States of America

Acknowledgments

With special thanks to:
Terry and Valerie Jensen and Kathy Farr.

Dedication

To the most wonderful hobo I never knew
-My Dad-

The Christmas Search

The waves of Lake Michigan had frozen in place. Permanent whitecaps reminded passers-by how harsh the winds of winter could be. Johnny sat down on a piece of driftwood and gazed at the sunset, turning from the reds and yellows and oranges into the drab gray which would beacon the cold dark of night. He pulled his jacket down to cover as much of his legs as possible and shoved his gloveless hands deep into the pockets. He was grateful his father's jacket was too large for him, giving more protection from the cold November air.

The waves crashed against the shore, tossing rushes back and forth against the shoreline and into each other. Like the rushes, Johnny felt completely out of control.

Soon the lake would be gripped by the frozen hand of hard winter, leaving the rushes frozen in place. Again he related his own life to them. He too felt as though he were frozen in life, unable to move from the grip of things over which he had no control.

The cold wind blew off the lake and into his face. He pulled his coat tightly and pulled his knees against his chest. The cold beating his body could not compare to the cold he felt inside.

Resting his head on his knees, he pondered how life had led him to this time and place. His mother had told him that all things happen for a reason. "Never have doubt, Johnny," she had said. "There is a reason for everything under the sun." Would she still feel that way? He wondered. What could have been the reason she had struggled raising Johnny and his little brother Joey after their father had died?

His mind drifted back to other times, times when he would stand by the gate, watching his father, covered with coal dust, come toward him in long strides. Unrecognizable by some, his fathers face was as blackened as the overalls he wore. Johnny however, could recognize that long stride from blocks away. Both he and his brother would anticipate their father's return from the coal mine each day.

He would pat Johnny on the head and throw Joey in the air. He would come home dirty and tired because, as he told Johnny, he was a working man, and the pride Johnny felt in his father made him want to be a working man too.

He wanted to work in a coal mine and come home dirty and tired just like his dad.

His dad had been his hero and nothing bad ever happened to a hero. When his father developed a cough, Johnny had believed he had a cold, but the coughing became worse. When his father missed a day of work to go to the doctor, Johnny was worried. His dad never missed work. Johnny had heard the word "tuberculosis" before, but as in most dreaded things in life, it only happened to others. Not this time. His father would be taken to a sanitarium, where he would stay until he died.

"What was the reason?" he had wanted to ask his mother, but he didn't. Nor did he ask the reason for their living in poverty on the meager living his mother had made cleaning houses, or the reason the depression hit, and she lost her job, and he had to quit school. Nor did he ask the reason for her dying and leaving him and Joey alone. Now Joey was ill.

He looked up at the sky changing into the dark gray of night, and with tears rolling down his cheeks he yelled at heaven. "WHY?" He wanted a reason!

The heavens remained silent. He sat alone waiting for an answer a while longer until he felt as though the cold had seeped into his bones and that he would never be warm again. He picked up the piece of driftwood and carried it back to the Jungle. It would burn. His walk hadn't been completely in vain.

*****

The news was that there were 250,000 teenagers riding the rails during this depression. Each toted an individual bag of problems. This hobo jungle was home to some of them, including him and Joey.

Johnny set the piece of driftwood next to the large metal barrel in front of the car. The fire was hot, making the metal can glow, as embers crackled and hissed, and the smoke floated toward the darkening sky. Members of their boxcar family hovered around it warming their hands as the melted snow below it ran past their feet.

Johnny looked around at the faces that were illuminated by the light of the burning barrel. Most of them were children, some younger and some older than Johnny. They all shared one thing in common. The "Big Trouble" as The Depression was called, had forced them out of their homes. All had headed out, trying to find work to earn enough to feed themselves and maybe enough to send back home to help their families. They talked of times before the "Big Trouble," when they were able to shine shoes, deliver papers or clean, to make a little money to help out, but then came the time when no one had money. There wasn't enough to buy coal for the stoves. A fire was started only long enough to fix some mush. When children became cold, they went to bed. Families were split, and dreams were lost.

His mind slipped back a couple of months. A bunch of them had gotten off the train at a small town hoping to find a job or maybe a handout. No sooner did their feet hit the ground, and the train pulled out, than the railroad bull and several others surrounded them. They held in their hands picks and shovels and clubs, ready to take on the group of young hobos. The sheriff arrived and told the kids that they were not welcome. He said he was going to take them to jail, and in the morning they were to catch the train to Chicago and never show their faces in his town again.

"I will see that you have a hot meal and a warm cot for the night," he said. "Then in the morning, you can have a hot breakfast and a shower and shave before you leave."

To the weary and hungry travelers, it didn't sound so bad. They followed with the sheriff, trailed by the railroad bull and his men, making sure the young hobos did not dart and escape.

Once inside the jail, their warm cot ended up being the cold concrete floor and the hot meal promised was a tin plate with cold tomatoes and a cold baked potato and moldy bread. Their hot breakfast was watered down mush served in the same dirty tin plate from the night before and another piece of the moldy bread. The jail inmates, however, those arrested for stealing or disturbing the peace, received bacon and eggs and hot coffee.

The next morning, they caught the train headed for Chicago, knowing they could all live better in a hobo jungle, depending upon each other, rather than taking the handouts of such kind people as the sheriff. It would be an unwritten rule that one would not panhandle or steal within a mile of the jungle. Once outside the radius of a mile, one could do what they needed in order to survive. Just don't bring trouble back with them. That was the rule of the Jungle.

*****

Johnny pulled back the heavy door and, with the lantern they shared, found Joey huddled in their corner. Johnny was grateful for the blankets they had been given by the mission.

"Hey, lazy bones, are you sleeping?" Johnny asked.

"No. I'm just pretending," Joey answered as Johnny reached down and tucked the covers under the neck of his little brother. He was burning up with fever, and his small body shivered from chills. Johnny reached over and piled what little clothing they had on top of Joey, hoping it would help to warm him. He remembered when he had called Joey "pest." Joey had followed him everywhere.

"Dad, make Joey stay home," he remembered saying. "He's always following me around."

"I guess he figures you're worth following," his dad replied. "It makes it kind of hard doesn't it son?"

"Makes what hard?"

"Knowing that your footsteps will influence your brother. You're his example. Make sure he follows you in the right direction."

"Where's the right direction, Dad?" Johnny's mind whispered. "How can you go in the right direction when you're lost?"

Then somewhere deep inside, whether it

was from his mind or his heart he heard the faintest reply. "Just keep doing right."

It seemed as if it were only yesterday that he walked the streets of their small town with his dad towering beside him. He kicked a rock along in front of him, to have his dad join in when he missed it. He could almost feel the warm sun that brightened the summer day.

The house water pump had decided to moan and screech, begging for attention that warm Saturday morning. They walked in the direction of the hardware store to find the parts his dad would need for repairs.

In front of them, a fine looking stranger walked out of the grocery store and got in a shiny black sedan. Johnny heard someone say, "That's Baby Face Nelson."

Johnny had heard of Baby Face Nelson. He was known to be part of Al Capone's group and despite his appearance was not one to be reckoned with.

"Dad." Johnny said. "What would make someone like him become a gangster?"

"Well, I heard that when he was a kid, he was teased about having a baby-face. I guess he felt he had to prove himself to someone, maybe himself. There's something I want you to remember, son. In this life, there will always be hurdles. Life isn't always fair but it gives you a choice. You can either take those hurdles and learn and grow from them, or you can use them to make you mad and bitter. One way or the other, you have the choice. I promise you this, though. If you learn and grow from what life places in your way, when you look back, you won't be sorry."

"I guess the trick is just to be a fast learner, " Johnny said looking up at his dad smiling.

His dad smiled back, put his hand on his shoulder, and quickly retrieved the escaping rock with the toe of his boot.

*****

"I have a little hot soup outside, Squirt. Do you think you could eat a little? I know your throat is sore, but you really should try, you know."

"I'll try, Johnny," Joey answered in his voice faint.

Johnny went back out and retrieved the soup he had warmed in a coffee can. He had diluted it with snow a little more than he should have, making it taste weak, but hopefully providing enough for another meal. He carried it in and propped Joey's head enough to ladle small spoonfuls into his mouth.

"Now, don't you think I'm about the best cook in the world?" Johnny asked, knowing full well his brother would have a different opinion.

"Are you sure it isn't warm rain water?" Joey chirped back weakly.

"Pretty much," Johnny answered, "but it will warm your innards anyway."

"Johnny. Isn't it about Thanksgiving time?" Joey asked.

Thanksgiving—Johnny hadn't even thought of it, but it was November, and although time had no meaning in their lives, holidays came around anyway.

"Remember our Thanksgiving the year before Dad went away?" Joey asked before coughing.

Johnny's mind drifted back to recall that Thanksgiving day that Joey talked about. They had gone with their dad wild turkey hunting and had bagged a nice tom. They had sat together on the log bench outside their house and picked the feathers until not a fluff could be found. Their mother had boiled the giblets and seasoned them with sage. She had made a cornbread dressing and yams they had grown in the small garden in back of their house.

He had been young, and although he was aware of Thanksgiving and being thankful, with youth sometimes things are taken for granted. He had eaten until he felt he would burst and then laid in front of the coal stove and read through a magazine that his dad had brought home from the mine. How he loved to read. Looking through any magazine he could find would take him to far away places and into dreams of wonderful things yet to come. He was a kid, and the world was his to be savored when-ever he felt like tasting, but this wasn't the world he had expected, and as for the tasting, it was very bitter.

"I remember, Joey," he answered to his brother's question.

"It was nice. Wasn't it? Johnny, do you think we will ever be happy again?"

"Well, what do you mean by that? You mean to say you're not happy seeing the world with your big brother? There you lie in a down-filled bed, eating pheasant under glass. All being served by, I must say, an extremely handsome and debonair waiter." He stood straight and paraded like a butler with a stick up his back bringing a soft chuckle from his small brother.

"Things are going to get better," he said as he continued giving Joey sips of soup. "The depression isn't going to last forever. When it is over, I will get a job in the mines, and we will get us a house. You will be able to go to school, and we will have turkey dinner again. I promise you."

"I don't need to go to school. I could get a job too."

"No, Joey. You need to go to school. Mama wanted us to go to school and so did Pa. He wanted us to have a better life than they had. You need to go to school for Mama and Pa and me too, Joey."

"Okay, Johnny. Whatever you say," Joey replied as he lay back down and curled up under the blankets and clothes. "Johnny, I promise, someday I won't be a pest."

"Yes you will," Johnny replied tousling his brother's hair. "That's what you kid brothers are meant to be. You're just doing your job."

Johnny walked back out into the cold night. He placed the piece of driftwood onto the fire and listened to it crackle and hiss. As the talk of the hobo jungle filled the air, he sipped on some of the soup, while a cold breeze blew snowflakes around his feet. He watched them disappear against the side of the fire barrel. They reminded him of his dreams, slowly disappearing.

Strange as it was, Johnny and Joey were among the most blessed in the Jungle. The boxcar, although shared by others like themselves, provided more shelter than the car bodies and boxes that most of the hobos lived in. The door could be closed and the winter winds locked outside. Had it not been for Old Joe, they might have been among the less fortunate. The boxcar had been Joe's home for several months, and so he claimed ownership. Johnny and Joey had been ones he had invited to share his "abode" as he called it.

Underneath Joe's straggly beard and dirty clothes was a gentleman waiting to emerge. Johnny looked around the jungle and wondered what lay beneath the surfaces of the others waiting to emerge. What was locked in so tightly by the depression? What parts of these hobos' characters had been replaced by shear survival instincts. Sometime, in another time and another place, when America was back on her feet, they might meet again. Maybe some would be doctors, lawyers, and merchants. As for Johnny, he would be a working man.

*****

The talk around camp was that there would be a food riot. The store at the south end of town was half-stocked with food, and there were hungry people needing it. Hunger can do strange things to people, especially when they watch their children crying. Some called the hobos savages. They weren't the savages. The savage was the depression, brought on by things totally beyond these people's control. They had no say in its birth and could only pray for its death. They could only try to survive its life. If begging, eating out of garbage cans or rioting were the only means of survival, then so be it. They would do what they needed to do.

Some of the victims of the depression had been bankers, some owned their own businesses, and some were laborers. There were an estimated 25,000 families wandering through the country looking for food, clothing, shelter and a job. There were more than 200,000 young people whose parents found it necessary to tell them they would have to fend for themselves—they could no longer be supported. How it must have broken the parents' hearts to send their children away.

The riot would be tomorrow. The cold

would overtake hunger tonight. They would stay in their makeshift shelters and huddle from the snow that was just starting to fall. Johnny had no choice; he would have to riot too. Joey needed food, something more than watered-down soup to help him regain his strength. More than that, he needed something to take his fever down.

The morning brought with it more cold and more hunger and, to Joey, the same fever that racked his body with chills. Johnny covered him again and told him to lie there, and he would be back. He would bring something to help him feel better.

The store would have opened at nine o'clock, but at eight the crowd was already there, sticks and rocks at hand. The first rock flew through a large pane window, taking out the signs that advertised the items they needed. A metal rod broke open the door, and the mob ran in just as the owner came down the stairs with his shotgun. Before he could get it to his shoulder he was attacked and hit over the head with a board, sending him crashing to the floor.

Items were pulled from the shelves. As quickly as they came, the rioters were gone. Holding a bottle of milk and a bag of eggs, Johnny stood next to the fallen storeowner. He leaned down and placed a wet towel on the head of the moaning man. The owner's eyes blinked as he tried to regain some sense of the madness.

"Where are they?" He asked.

"They're gone," Johnny replied.

"Where did they go?" the owner asked again.

"Who knows?" Johnny answered. "There are a lot of hungry people around. They could have gone anyplace."

"Are you one of them?" the storekeeper asked as he tried to position himself to a sitting position.

"Yeah. I was one of them, one of the hungry ones."

"Well, why didn't you take off with them?"

"I just wanted to make sure you were all right."

"Well, you might as well take off. That bag of eggs and can of milk isn't enough to keep my market open for."

"Could I trade them?" Johnny asked hesitantly.

"Trade them for what?" the storekeeper questioned.

"For some aspirin," Johnny answered.

"Why do you need aspirin? I'm the one with the headache," the storekeeper replied rubbing the growing goose egg on his head.

"My little brother has a bad fever. I need some aspirin for him to take the fever down."

The storekeeper struggled to his feet as Johnny positioned the shotgun, enabling the owner to use it to keep his balance.

"Where're your parents?" The storekeeper asked.

"Ain't got any. They both died." Johnny replied with the truth, but not wanting sympathy.

"So you're in charge of your brother, huh?"

"Seems so." Johnny answered.

The storekeeper shuffled to a shelf where the aspirin was kept and handed Johnny a bottle.

"Here," he said, shoving them toward Johnny.

"Here's your eggs and milk," Johnny

replied.

"Oh, just keep them," the storekeeper answered. "As I said, they're not enough to keep my store opened for."

"Thanks," Johnny replied. "I'll go feed my brother and give him some aspirin and then I'll come back and help clean this up," he said looking at the broken glass and overturned shelves.

"Thanks, again," he said to the storekeeper who brushed him off with a wave of his hand.

Back at the Jungle people were feeding their children and themselves, being careful not to be extravagant with their stolen food. It would have to last.

Johnny pulled back the door to the boxcar and found Joey as he had left him, still fevered and chilling.

"Here. Take this," Johnny said as he handed an aspirin to Joey. "Mama used to give these to us when we were sick."

Joey swallowed the aspirin along with some water from melted snow.

"I'll be back in a few minutes with a cooked egg for you."

"Where did you get an egg?" Joey asked

as Johnny opened the door again.

"It was given to us," he answered, not being untruthful.

He did, as he had promised, go back to the store and help clean up the results of the riot. The storekeeper had put a bandage on the bump on his head and tried to help, but would become dizzy each time he leaned over. Johnny was glad to do something to undo some of the damage done.

"You and your brother should be in an orphanage." The storekeeper said. "At least you would have a place to stay and some food to eat."

"I promised Mama that I would take care of Joey," Johnny said. "If they put us in an orphanage, chances are we'd be separated and that we might never see each other again. I can't let that happen. He's my brother."

The storekeeper acted like Johnny wasn't using his head, and Johnny felt the storekeeper wasn't using his heart. Chances were, both were right, but matters of the head are easier to dismiss than matters of the heart. Johnny would take care of Joey.

*****

Johnny found a newspaper the next day.

The front page recapped the story of the riot and warned other storekeepers to be on guard. The interview with the storekeeper revealed he didn't blame the rioters. They were poor unfortunate souls who needed food and medicine. His understanding was appreciated. For a while, the Jungle would survive on what food they had stolen and what they could forage from the garbage cans. The missions and the charities were running low. There was little to be had.

The aspirin helped Joey. It didn't take away the sickness, but it did make it easier for him to bear. November came and left as it had entered, cold and hopeless. December brought with it a blizzard that lasted for two days. Blowing snow piled up around the boxcar and the other shanties in the hobo jungle. Residents wrapped rags around their feet and hands and heads to ward off the penetrating cold. Some had caught the train and headed for what they hoped to be warmer climates. Johnny couldn't leave while Joey was sick. They would stay in the box-car and hope that the storm would subside, and, in a figment of their imaginations, things would get better.

Johnny left Joey that December morning with Old Joe's promise to look in on him. He was going into town to see if there was any food, clothes or rags that could be found, or anything else that could be of use to those at the hobo jungle. Would anyone think that an old rag they threw out could be used to ward off the cold from a little girl's ears, or that scraps of food, which they would never consider eating, could be relished by another?

The blizzard had subsided and left in its place large fluffy snowflakes floating to the ground in complete silence. In his youth, Johnny would have enjoyed the opportunity of building snowmen, or sliding down the hill behind their house, and sliding across frozen puddles. A surprise attack of snowballs against the Dawson brothers would bring about a snowball war between all the boys of their mining community. He remembered, with a smile, the time he had accidentally (as he had told the story) hit his Dad in the back of his head with a snowball as he had walked home from work. His dad wasted no time in getting revenge by burying him in a large snow bank.

Where had his youth gone? He felt so very old.

Johnny felt unshed tears sting his eyes. He struggled to change his memories to keep the tears from flowing uncontrollably.

"All things happen for a reason," he heard his mother whisper to him again. His heart was beginning to harden a little at that theory.

He had held her hand and it had felt cold, not cool like the countless times she had placed it on his fevered brow. He was told he had to be brave. He had to be a man, he was told by those who had visited. So he sat at the head of her bed and held back his tears and held back his fear as she whispered. "Everything happens for a reason."

"Take care of Joey for me, sweetheart," she had said.

"I will, Mama," Johnny had replied.

"Remember, darling." Her voice was strained. "God is just a whisper away."

Joey had cried himself to sleep that night. Johnny lay awake and listened to the well-meaning voices trying to decide his and Joey's lives.

"We'll need to call the child services," the minister said. "Perhaps they can find homes for the boys."

"No one will be able to take them both," a neighbor spoke up. "No one can afford two extra mouths to feed. It will be hard enough to find anyone who can take in one."

The tears flowed freely down Johnny's face as he heard his mother's voice once more.

"Take care of Joey for me, sweetheart."

Again, Johnny reaffirmed, "I will, Mama."

They had left the cemetery together. Johnny held tightly to Joey's hand and tried to assure him that everything was going to be all right.

Johnny had packed a few of their belongings before the services. He had been careful to only select those items he and Joey could carry.

"Do you trust me, Joey?" Johnny asked.

"Sure I do, Johnny," his little brother replied.

"Then we need to run away. If we don't, we might get separated and never see each other again."

Joey had answered by picking up his belongings. Together they walked out the back door. They had stopped once to look back, to say good-bye. Good-bye to their dad, and to their mom, and to their childhoods.

*****

Johnny walked behind the diner at the

edge of town. There were some burnt pancakes that had been thrown out along with a small jar of bacon grease. He folded the pancakes in a piece of newspaper and shoved the bottle of bacon grease into his pocket. Down the road, he passed a white house with blue windowsills. A white picket fence separated it from the road, and smoke rose from the chimney. Frosted windows displayed the artwork of winter, as hanging icicles glistened in the December sun. It looked as though it would be a kind place, so he timidly walked toward the front door. Upon his knocking, a young girl about his age answered. She seemed neither surprised by his appearance nor that he would be knocking on their door.

"May I help you?" she asked.

"Would you have any food you could spare?" He replied, finding himself suddenly embarrassed by his appearance and his begging.

Her eyes were dark brown as was her hair, which was secured by gold barrettes behind her ears and left to fall down her back. She was beautiful, and for a moment he felt like making a mad dash to get as far away as possible, but then he remembered Joey.

"Anything you might be able to spare would be appreciated."

"Just a minute. I'll check with my mother," she answered, as she walked away turning to look over her shoulder at him.

She returned a few minutes later with a bag of bread and honey sandwiches.

"Here is a bottle of milk and some sandwiches. The bread is fresh. My mother just made it this morning," she said, not knowing that in his pocket were two burnt pancakes and that freshness wasn't a priority.

"Thank you," he said, feeling conscientious that—as he reached for the bag with his dirty hand—he almost touched her.

"Have a good day," she said as he turned to leave.

If anyone else had told him to have a good day, anger would have overtaken him. How could you have a good day when you lived in a hobo jungle, when both of your parents were dead, when you had a young brother to care for and when you were begging for food? Her saying it was more of a confirmation, however, that he would have a good day and so he smiled.

"Thank you," he said as he ducked his head and turned away to the sound of the door closing.

He closed the picket gate behind him and saw her looking at him through the curtains. Again, he felt uncomfortable and took quick long strides to escape her gaze.

Johnny walked along the streets staring into the empty storefront windows. He passed the schoolhouse and listened to the emptiness. Even the schools were closed. Some of them were only opened for sixty days a year. The rest of them were closed entirely. There was no consolation in knowing that the entire world was in a depression. The newspapers wrote that Germany was looking toward a new Chancellor, one who would save them. His name was Adolf Hitler.

When the mission was a short distance away, Johnny could see the line of people stretching halfway down the block. He hoped that perhaps he could find a warmer coat for Joey and perhaps a pair of used shoes without holes in the soles that might fit him. He would wait in line.

From somewhere, perhaps from within the mission, came the sound of music. Johnny strained to listen to sounds of the season. He had forgotten about Christmas. Somehow, in the battle to survive, some things were forgotten. He listened to the gentle strains of violin music playing

"Silent Night." Again, for a moment, his thoughts returned him to happier times.

He could almost feel the warmth of the kitchen and smell the raisin bread that his mother baked to take to an elderly couple that lived down the road. Mr. Moore had been ill, and Johnny's mother had put together a gift basket of raisin bread and bottled preserves. He could remember looking out their window and seeing the windowpane decorated in frost almost as though winter had taken a brush and painted it especially for their pleasure.

Papa and Mama, Johnny and Joey had all pulled on their boots and with Papa carrying the basket trudged through the snow to the Moores' home. Once on the step, they sang a Christmas carol and left the basket with the Moores. He remembered how warm he felt inside, even though the temperature was dropping. He wished he could capture that feeling once again and the warmth of knowing all was well.

He had worked his way to the mission door. There were no boots or shoes to fit Joey but there was a coat, a very used, but heavy jacket that would surely help keep him warm. He tucked it under his coat to keep it dry and headed back toward the boxcar.

On the corner stood a few cut Christmas trees. The sign said 50 cents a tree. Only a selected few would enjoy the smell and sight of a decorated Christmas tree this year. As he walked by, the scent of pine floated in the cold air.

He sat down upon a wooden bench and gazed at the tall pine tree across the street, watching the December wind force its boughs to dance to the music of the mission bells. He remembered how it felt, having the Christmas spirit. He remembered the warmth of it, the excitement of it. How he wanted to have it back. Where had it been lost? Was it left in the warmth of his childhood home? Did his mother and father take it with them? Was it left with his lost childhood, unable to be found and recaptured? He closed his eyes tight and tried to will it into his spirit but opened them to find only emptiness inside. "Where's it at?" he asked himself as he stood and faced toward the wind. All he heard in answer was silence to his question.

He tucked his thoughts away to step back into reality. They would have to be explored another day. Joey was waiting.

*****

Joey lay curled up into a tight ball. He didn't want to straighten his legs, knowing that the cold of the worn blankets would be there to greet them. He shivered and tucked his nose under trying to warm it. His skin was sore from the fever and, with each small move, hurt against the covers. His joints ached, and he would drift off to sleep to be awakened by the burning of his throat. He could hear the sounds of the hobo jungle seeping into the boxcar. He tried to think of pleasant things to keep his mind off the cold and pain. He wasn't certain if his thoughts were memories or merely remnants of dreams. Whatever they were, he liked them. He thought of home, the memory of pulling warm taffy with Johnny and sliding the pan across the top of the coal stove waiting for the popcorn to pop. He remembered the town park. He could almost picture himself walking across the snow-covered ground with one hand tucked inside his mother's and the other in his father's, watching his breath puff into the night air. He could see the platform ahead, and the line of children waiting their turn to sit on the lap of the red-suited gentleman handing out candy canes and listening to wishes. In his memories, he could feel it! The excitement mingled with mystery. Then there was the other feeling, the warm feeling he felt as they watched Johnny and the group of children as they sang "Silent Night." For some reason the feeling made him want to cry, not from sorrow, but for happiness.

He could only capture the feelings in his memories, for when he slipped back to reality, they were gone, hiding like lost friends in places he knew not where to seek. They had to be out there someplace. Maybe they were outside the Jungle. Maybe outside they could be found and captured and tucked back into his heart, where they would be treasured.

The lump in his throat made it hurt worse, but he couldn't help it. He missed his Mom and Dad. He wanted to feel warm inside again. How he wanted to kneel beside his bed and have his father and mother listen to his prayers and then jump into bed and be covered with the patchwork quilts his mother had made. He would feel his dad tousle his hair and the kiss of his mother on his cheek as they wished him "good-night." He tasted the tear as it slipped onto his parched lips. He was glad he had Johnny.

His mind slipped back into reality as Old Joe slid the door to the boxcar open. "I thought you might be awake," he said to Joey. "Here. Let me slide this warm rock down by your feet. I warmed it in the fire and wrapped it up in newspapers. It should take some of the chill out of your bed."

Joey stretched his feet down and found the warmth. "Thank you, Joe," he said. "Joe, have you always been a hobo?" he asked as the rugged old man straightened his shoulders back and slid his hands into the pockets of his worn jacket.

"Well, believe it or not," Joe answered, "before you stands a gentleman butler. I have served in the homes of many well fortuned families. That was before the plight befell them. That was when I was addressed as Joseph. I have managed the households of many of the once rich," he said, as he brushed away a speck of lint from his worn lapel.

"It must be nice being rich," Joey answered wistfully.

"Having money has its benefits, young Joey," Joe replied, "but it doesn't necessarily make one rich. As I said, I have served in the homes of many well-fortuned families, but few would I truly consider rich. I have seen many who have based their own self worth upon how many possessions they owned. They felt the more they acquired, the more was their personal worth. The depression has been a sad lesson to many. Many have been forced to learn that basing one's own value upon how much one owns is a fallacy. Many have lost their riches, and by not having their priorities properly placed, have lost themselves also. No, few do I truly consider rich."

"Then who is rich?" Joey asked, confused by Old Joe's remarks.

"You're rich, Joey, and so is your brother, not by what the world might consider rich, but by what truly matters. You both have been loved and have the capacity to love. You both recognize the value of family, even though you two are the only family you have. You both have kind hearts and gentle spirits. The depression came, but was unable to rob you of your riches because you held that which is of everlasting value, that which is unable to be torn or tarnished, stolen or broken. You and Johnny are rich. Someday, when the depression ends, you will see that you have carried your riches with you into the future.

"Are you rich?" Joey asked.

"Oh, yes, I am a very rich man, for I have dreams. One day I will again offer my services to someone who will appreciate a person of my dignity," Joe said bending low at his waist. "Now, you get some rest. I'll see if I can find another warm rock for your bed."

Joey stretched his feet, trying to surround the warmth in the bottom of his bed. He hoped Old Joe was right. He drifted off to sleep with hope.

*****

Johnny crossed the river and followed it toward Lake Michigan and the community of tramps where he and Joey lived. He could hear their voices float in the cold December air. "What would become of them all?" His mind questioned. "Would they survive? Where would they be next month or next year? Will any of their dreams come true?" He remembered once more something that his mother had told him. "Yesterday is the past. Tomorrow may not come. Today is the present. It is a gift." For now, he would not worry about tomorrow. He would not pine for what was past. He would live today.

Old Joe stood at the barrel warming his hands over the burning corncobs that he had brought from the stockyards.

"He's been very sick today," he said, anticipating Johnny's question. " I gave him another aspirin to take his fever down. He wouldn't eat anything, though. He said that his throat is much too sore. He really needs to receive some nourishment."

"Thanks for looking after him, Joe. I have

some honey sandwiches, if you would like one."

"That would be a pleasure," Joe said in his English butler voice.

Johnny slid the door to the boxcar open, careful not to spill the precious can of warmth he held.

"Hey, lazy bones, here's a little warm milk for you. I know your throat is sore, but you need to drink a little, and by the way, I have a present for you."

"What?" asked Joey, positioning himself on an elbow to sip the milk.

Johnny pulled the jacket from underneath his coat and helped Joey put it on.

"There. That will keep you warmer. It's only temporary you know. Someday, you are going to have the warmest wool coat with gloves and a scarf for your neck to match. Of course, you will have new boots too, and, who knows, you might even have silk underwear."

"I'll only wear silk underwear, if you do." Joey replied.

"Not me!" Johnny said. "I'm afraid they might slip right off."

A small chuckle came from Joey as

Johnny sat down next to him to tell him of his day in town. He told him of the girl at the house, the one that had given them the sandwiches and milk, and of hearing the Christmas music at the mission. He told him of the Christmas tree lot and the smell of the pine.

"I wish I could go with you," Joey said. "Maybe I could find it in town?"

"Find what?" Johnny asked

"The feeling," Joey answered, "The feeling I used to feel at Christmas time. You think I'm being dumb don't you?"

"No, Joey. I don't think you're being dumb," Johnny answered, remembering trying to will the spirit of Christmas back into his own heart.

"You'll be able to soon," replied Johnny. "Just try and get to feeling better."

*****

The days came and went, and there was no improvement in Joey. His throat hurt so badly and he spat up blood when he coughed. The aspirin were used quickly. There was no use in taking Joey to the hospital. They only accepted local residents.

Again, Johnny walked down toward the

lake. He sat down on a rock, and his mind whirled. His little brother was too sick for him to care for. He needed more help than anyone in the hobo jungle could provide. He could not afford to take him to the doctor. He couldn't take him to the hospital. There was only one solution. He would have to take Joey to the orphanage. His mind ached, and his heart felt as though it would break in two at that thought. He had promised his mother that he would take care of Joey, and now it had come to this. He would take him to the orphanage, and he probably would never see his little brother again. He would not fulfill any of his promises to him that he had made.

He hated this life. He hated the present. It was no gift, as his mother had told him. It was a stomach full of hurt. Who made him the master of his fate and that of Joey's? Who had gotten his permission to be in charge? He hadn't asked for it, and God knew he didn't want it. He wanted to be young. He wanted to have the security of his dad and the warmth of his mother. He wanted to go to school and play baseball and dream of young girls, perhaps the one in the white house with the picket fence. He didn't want to be in charge. He didn't want to make the decisions. He just wanted to be young. Again, within his mind, his mother's voice came saying, "There is a reason for everything under the sun."

"I don't believe you, Mama," he said with tears now flowing uncontrollably down his cheeks. "How could there be a reason for this? I love Joey, and now I am going to abandon him in an orphanage. I don't know where I'm going or what I'll be when I get there. I just wanted to be a working man."

He sat there, looking across the frozen lake. He remembered his mother and "The Lord's Prayer" that she had taught them to say. Every night after they had gone to bed, he would hear her recite the prayer, and after she would finish, he would whisper the same. She had found such comfort in that prayer. Even after their father had died, she would recite it each night and be renewed in faith that all would be well. Johnny had never found that comfort. To him, it was just a bunch of words, some of which he didn't understand, but in the cold of the night he found himself whispering once more.

"Our Father which art in Heaven, hallowed be thy name. Thy Kingdom come. Thy will be done, in Earth as it is in Heaven. Give us this day our daily bread and forgive us our debts as we forgive our debtors. And lead us not into temptation, but deliver us from evil. For thine is the kingdom, and the power and the glory. Forever. Amen."

"God," he cried. "If you are somewhere out there, then why have you abandoned us? Have I done something so bad that you don't see what's going on? Why do you let this happen to people? Where were you when my dad got sick? Where were you when my mom died? Where are you now when so many people are hurting and hungry and cold? Where are you tonight when Joey is lying in there sick and needs help? WHERE ARE YOU?"

Again the heavens heard the cry of an anguished boy, and again they remained silent.

He sat by the lake and cried until his head ached, and he felt there were no more tears inside. He would sit a while longer and wait for the swelling in his eyes to go down, so Joey would not know he had been crying. Then he would go back to the boxcar. Tomorrow he would carry his little brother to the orphanage. "At least," he thought, "tomorrow night Joey will sleep in a cot and have some hot soup in his belly. He will have the medicine he needs to get better, and maybe someone will take him into their home and give him a future. He will be better off without me. I'm sure that Dad and Mom would think so, too.

*****

As much as he tried to convince himself, his heart continued to ache, and once again the Heavens heard his silent prayer, "Please God help me."

Slowly and silently, he walked back to the boxcar. He had never felt so alone. He reached his hand inside his collar and pulled out a chain. Attached to it was half of a family crest. Again memories of his mother flooded his mind. As she had lain in bed, she had given the chain and half crest to him.

"Take this Johnny. It was your father's. Keep it close to your heart. Remember always that the poor can be rich, and the rich can be poor. Sometimes the hardest thing to hold onto is faith, but faith precedes miracles."

She hadn't explained herself. She simply closed her eyes and fell asleep. He figured she had meant the depression. The rich too had become poor, but that didn't account for what she meant when she said the poor can be rich, and how did her faith create miracles for her?

"I don't understand, Mama," he said looking up at the dark sky. "I don't understand," he whispered above the ache in his throat. Maybe it was a secret she believed in, like she believed there was a reason for everything. Whatever it was, it was a secret, because Johnny didn't understand any of it.

He slid back the door to the boxcar. The ray of the evening's last sunlight shone across to where Joey lay. Johnny went to check on him, only to find him awake.

"How are you feeling, Squirt?" he asked as he sat down on the bed next to Joey, trying hard to disguise the hurt in his heart.

"I'm okay, Johnny. Old Joe says that today is Christmas Eve. Is it?"

"I guess it is, Joey. I've kind of lost track of time, but if Old Joe says it is, then it must be."

"Johnny, I know I've been a pest for you, but would you do me a favor?"

"What's that, Joey?"

"Take me out to find Christmas."

"What do you mean, find Christmas?"

"I don't know, Johnny. If it's Christmas Eve, then Christmas has got to be out there. The feeling we used to get when Dad and Mom were alive. I want to find it so badly. Please Johnny. Let's go find Christmas before it's too late."

As sick as Joey had been and for all that they had gone through together, Johnny had never remembered Joey asking for anything. He had just accepted what had happened to their father and mother and had never complained about being hungry or cold or sick. Would he be able to accept going into the orphanage the same way? This was the first time he had asked for anything, but what was he asking for? Where do you go looking for Christmas? Where could the spirit they knew be found again?

Maybe if Johnny took him to the Christmas tree lot or to the mission to hear the Christmas music, then maybe that would be what he meant by going to find Christmas. Whatever it meant, Johnny would take Joey out to find it. This would be the last one they'd spend together, and he didn't want Joey to remember it as lying in the boxcar. If Joey wanted to go out to find Christmas, then that is what they would do. Where they would find it was anyone's guess.

"Are you sure you feel well enough to do this?" Johnny asked Joey as he struggled to put on his shoes.

"I'm sure, Johnny. If you can just help me a little, I'm sure I can make it."

His face was flushed, and his skin hot. He

really should rest and not exert himself, but Johnny didn't have the heart to deny his wish.

"Put that old sweater on under your jacket. It will keep you a little warmer."

Joey slid his arm into the sleeve of his coat and buttoned the buttons up to the top. Johnny slid a rag around Joey's neck and into the front of his collar to keep the wind from blowing the snow into his clothes.

"Here," he said stooping down. "Get on my back, and I will carry you."

Joey straddled Johnny's back as Old Joe opened the boxcar door.

Johnny stepped out into the December night. He was surprised at how warm it seemed. Large snowflakes fell in a never-ending tumble as they headed toward town. Again the thought of the orphanage entered Johnny's mind, and suddenly the weight on his back was light in comparison to the weight on his shoulders. He brushed the thoughts aside, for, tonight they were in search of Christmas.

*****

The sound of church bells was barely audible as they headed toward town, but with each step the chiming grew louder and clearer as

Johnny walked toward the church steeple point-ing toward the heavens in front of him. Surely, there they would find Christmas. In front of the church Johnny set Joey down on a bench, first dusting the snow from the seat with his arm.

A nativity scene sat just below the steps of the church. One could tell it had been used over and over, as the paint was chipped. Joseph and Mary looked down at the small babe lying in the manger.

Joey searched the eyes of each member of the nativity. Somewhere the spirit of Christmas could be found. He waited for the spirit to once again find him, but he felt nothing except a chill seeping down his back.

"Are you all right?" Johnny asked Joey.

"I'm fine, Johnny," Joey said as he looked first up one side of the street and then the other, only to see the darkness of the night interrupted by snowflakes. There were no Christmas lights or Christmas Scenes. There was only darkness and silence, except for the bells.

Both boys sat quietly on the bench. Neither of them felt anything that resembled the spirit of Christmas. Apparently, they had not found it here and would have to look further.

"Come on, Joey," Johnny said. "Let's keep going. Can you make it back on my back?"

"Just let me walk," Joey said. "I'm sure if you just help me, I can make it okay."

Johnny positioned his hand under Joey's elbow, and together they walked down the dark street, two shadows in search of the Christmas spirit they had felt as boys in front of the Moores' home. How do you search for something that had come so naturally before? Where do you search? Where can it be captured? Neither boy knew.

As they walked, Johnny's mind was full of tomorrow. How would he explain to Joey that he needed to take him to the orphanage? Would he understand that it was in his best interest? He needed to have a warm bed in which to sleep and warm food to eat. He needed a doctor to provide the medicine needed for him to get well. Logically, it made so much sense. Then why did his heart hurt so? He had been thinking of Joey, but now, for an instant, another thought crossed his mind. What about Johnny? For the first time he realized that after tomorrow, he would be alone, completely alone. Caring for Joey had made it easier to make decisions. He would do what he needed to do for Joey, but now what would he do? Suddenly, he felt as if he were one of the snowflakes being tossed aimlessly in the night by a December breeze. He would have nowhere to go and no one to go with. He would wander in life with no direction or purpose. When one has no dream, life loses its meaning. How could he catch hold of his dream, when he was living in a nightmare? What was the reason?

His thoughts were interrupted by Joey's frail voice.

"Look, Johnny" Joey said pointing to a horse drawn sleigh. Two lanterns hung above the figures sitting inside it, illuminating them in their fine attire and the warm, wool comforters protecting them. The bells around the horses' necks jingled. With each trot, the horses' hooves scattered snowflakes swirling about their feet. Laughter floated in the air above them.

"Where do you think they're going?" Joey asked Johnny.

"I don't know," he replied.

The two boys stopped for a moment, their gaze following the sleigh. It was only a moment that another followed. Again they heard laughter, intertwining with the song of "Jingle Bells."

"Let's follow them," Joey said. "Let's see where they're going!"

"You're too sick to go too far," Johnny said, feeling his brother's weight grow heavier on his hand as he supported Joey's elbow.

"Just help me, Johnny. They must know where Christmas is."

"All right, but get on my back again. If you get too heavy, I will let you walk some more, but you need to keep your strength."

Again, Joey straddled Johnny's back. "I'm sorry, Johnny."

"What are you sorry for?"

"I'm sorry to be such a pest." Joey answered, a little out of breath.

"Don't you know? That's what kid brothers are supposed to be. Like I said, you're just doing your job," Johnny chided. "Let's go see where they're going."

Johnny carried Joey down two blocks and then followed the sleighs as they ascended a winding road leading to Manor Hill. At the base of the hill Johnny stopped long enough to get his breath. And then, carefully, so as not to slip with his brother, he continued step by careful step. Again, his mind slipped towards tomorrow, and the weight on his shoulders became more than the weight on his back.

Two large wrought iron gates stood open at the top of the hill, awaiting the coming of the Christmas guests. Large lanterns twinkled in the night, showing off the holly decorating the fence and gates. On both sides hung large Christmas wreaths of pine bows and cranberries and red ribbons. Music floated in the air, and the most wonderful aroma filled the winter night.

"I think we've found it," Joey said. "I think we've found Christmas."

Carefully, Johnny slipped inside the gates, and sneaking from bush to tree to bush again, made his way toward the mansion on the hill.

The large windows in the front were decorated with frost, but the boys could still see, from a distance, that inside a wonderful party was going on.

Johnny carefully carried Joey to the side of the house where another large window was decorated with pine bows and ribbons. A candle illuminated it.

"Here," Johnny said, laying his coat out on the snow behind a tall bush. "Sit down here, and you can see through the window."

Johnny carefully held onto his brother, as

he helped him down upon the coat. He could feel the fever of Joey's body seeping through his clothes. He placed his hand on Joey's head, which instantly reflected the dry heat of a high temperature. He now noticed the swelling in Joey's face and hands. Why hadn't he seen it before? Panic gripped him, and he felt the hurt build just below his heart. He looked up toward the cold December heaven and silently prayed, "Please help us."

"I don't want your coat, Johnny. You'll get cold," Joey said, straining to force the words from his aching throat.

"I'm all heated up from carrying you up the hill," Johnny said. "Besides, I don't want you to get wet, and then I'll have a wet back when I carry you back down the hill. Really, I'm warm enough."

Joey strained to look through the window and marveled at the scene. The long winding stairway was decorated with garlands and large gold balls. A graceful Christmas tree stood in the corner reaching all the way to the ceiling. Small lit candles illuminated the decorations. The light shone on the gifts below, wrapped and tied in the most beautiful of wraps and bows. There was a long table filled with wonderful food: leg of lamb,

Christmas goose and turkey with all the trimmings including candied-yams, oyster dressings, cranberries—all that a person could dream of. Another table waited filled with chocolate cake, carrot cake, bread puddings, sugar cookies and assorted pies.

The guests dined and laughed and danced to a small orchestra playing the Christmas carols that both boys had heard—it seemed—so long ago.

Joey shivered, and Johnny reached down and pulled his coat up around his shoulders. The love he had for his brother had gone unspoken. For a moment his mind marveled at the fact that, although he had been responsible for Joey's every need since their parents had died, his sacrifice had only increased his love for his small brother. His throat ached with the thought of leaving him tomorrow. It ached with the realization of how ill his little brother was. It ached with the thought that he might lose his brother as he had lost his parents. The ache became unbearable.

The strains of "Silent Night" drifted in the frosty air. Silently Johnny whispered to the heavens, "Please God, help Joey. He's a good boy. He has never complained. He has slept in the cold and eaten garbage. He has accepted his life without ever asking why. He has given up his pa and ma and still holds onto his smile. He is losing the sparkle in his eyes, but only because he is so sick. I've failed him God, and I don't know what to do. If You can hear my prayer in the midst of all the others that are hurting and calling out to You, then please help Joey. I just don't know what to do"

Joey didn't notice the tears as Johnny wiped them away with the sleeve of his coat.

*****

"What are you doing out here?" The voice came from behind them. "This is no place for tramps."

Johnny turned to see a young man standing. He had on a top hat and a wool coat that came to his knees, with a collar of fur. Black leather gloves protected his hands, which he had set on his hips. And he wore shiny black boots on his feet. He was standing in a military stance.

"Answer me! What are you doing here? What are you planning on stealing?" His voice became louder, his face redder with each word.

"Answer me! What are you doing here?"

"What's going on?" Another voice came

from behind the young man.

"They're tramps, Uncle," the younger man said. "I caught them here, probably looking to see what they can steal."

"We're not here to steal anything," Johnny said defensively.

"You expect us to believe that?" the young man said. "I'll go call the police, Uncle. They can haul them back to their slums where they belong."

"Just wait, Emerson," the older man replied looking down at Joey.

"Please Sir, don't be angry with Johnny. It's all my fault. I asked him to take me to find Christmas and he brought me here. He didn't do anything wrong. It's my fault." Joey tried to continue but was interrupted by a cough that took away his breath.

"I'll take my brother and leave," Johnny said. "We weren't intending on stealing anything."

"That's all you tramps know how to do, is steal," Emerson broke in. "Uncle, let me call the police."

"Go back to the party, Emerson. I'll take care of this," the older gentleman replied.

Emerson huffed and turned sharply on his polished boot, then stormed back to the party.

"What's the matter with your brother?" the gentleman asked Johnny.

"He's been very sick," Johnny replied. "I don't know what is wrong with him. We can't take him to the hospital and we can't afford a doctor. They only help the locals."

"What is your name again?"

"My name is Johnny."

"And what is your brother's name?"

"Joey, sir," Johnny answered respectfully.

"Well, Johnny. I'm Jesse McCardy and this is my home. Help me get Joey up and into the house. A boy this sick shouldn't be sitting in the snow."

Johnny picked Joey up in his arms and the gentleman picked up the coat and shook the snow from it.

Johnny followed him into the house. Once they were inside, a tall, slim butler met them at the door.

"Charles, help get this boy to the guest

room," Jesse said, handing the boys' belongings to the butler.

"Yes, Sir," the butler replied.

"You're not bringing those tramps into the house, are you?" Emerson asked indignantly. "They will steal all they can get their hands on."

"This is my house, Emerson, and I will do whatever I please. Go back to the party and see to our guests until I return."

Charles took Joey from Johnny's arms and carried him up the winding staircase. Johnny followed.

*****

The covers were turned back on the four-posted bed. Charles laid Joey on it and pulled the covers up over him. He then lit the fire in the fireplace and pulled the heavy curtain closed to help warm the room.

Johnny stood in the corner, not touching anything for fear he would get it dirty. Joey began to cough again. He tried to catch his breath, but the coughing increased. Johnny went to his side and handed Joey the rag he had put around his neck. The rag was soaked through with red blood.

Charles entered carrying a tray with a

pitcher of water. He poured a glass, and Johnny held Joey's head while he sipped. The coughing subsided.

"Thank you," Johnny said to Charles.

"You're welcome," Charles replied. "Is there anything else I can get you?"

"No, thank you," Johnny answered surprised at the respect he was given.

"The doctor will be here soon, " Jesse said as he entered the room. "I sent the stable boy for him and told him it was urgent."

"We have no money to pay him," Johnny replied.

"Don't worry about that. Your brother needs a doctor, and a doctor he is going to have."

Johnny reached his hand down his shirt and from around his neck brought out a chain. On the chain hung the gold crest that had been cut in half. His father had worn the chain up until the day he died. He said it had been handed down from his father, and now it was handed down to Johnny. He knew nothing about the half crest, only that it had been his father's and now it was his. Except for the oversize coat he wore, it was all that he had left of his father.

"Here," he said handing the chain and half crest to the gentleman. "It's not worth much, but maybe it will help."

Jesse reached out and took what was handed him. Holding the chain in the air, the half crest dangled. A puzzled look came over his face.

"Where did you get this?" he questioned.

"It was my father's," Johnny replied. He left it to me when he died. It's not worth much money. I promise, though, I will repay you for whatever it takes for the doctor. I don't have a job right now, but I will have, and I will pay you back every penny. If I don't, then my father's crest is yours, but please, sir, if it's all right, would you keep it and give me a chance to earn it back? One day I'm going to be a working man like my father. Then I will pay you."

Jesse tucked the chain and crest inside his vest pocket. "I will keep it until you repay me, but until then, as I said, don't worry about it. When was the last time the two of you had something to eat? Why don't you get washed up, and I will have the cook bring up a tray?"

"You don't need to do that, Sir," Johnny replied. "Well, it would be good if Joey ate, to get his strength, but you've already done enough. I can wait until I get home."

"And just where is home?" Jesse asked.

"We live down by the lake," Johnny replied.

"They live in a hobo jungle," Emerson's voice came behind his Uncle. "And they're not to be trusted. They are probably planning on what they are going to steal now." He squared his shoulders and stood arrogantly in the doorway.

"Emerson," the uncle replied, "I thought I told you to go and see to our guests. You're not needed here."

"I was concerned for your safety, Uncle. It's not safe taking in tramps."

"My safety is my concern, Emerson. I have managed to take care of myself for many years without your help. I'm sure I can continue to do so. Please go back down to the party. Let your mother know I will be down shortly."

Emerson turned quickly and stormed off.

"It's not my safety he's concerned about, but rather my money," Jesse said.

"We wouldn't steal anything from you," Johnny said defensively. "The only thing I have ever taken without paying for was some food, but most of it was from the garbage cans. I give you my word, we won't steal from you."

"The food you are going home to eat, is it from garbage cans?" Jesse asked.

Johnny looked at the floor and then into the eyes of Jesse. "Yes," he said meekly.

"As I said before," Jesse continued, "get washed up, and I will have the cook bring a tray to you and your brother. You can eat from the garbage can another day," he said as he turned and walked from the room.

*****

Johnny walked into the adjoining bathroom. White towels hung from golden towel hooks. Small balls of soap sat in silver bowls on the countertop. He looked at himself in the gold-framed mirror that hung just above the sink and struggled to recognize the person staring back at him. His hair was oily and hung uncombed about his face, which was smudged with dirt. The shirt and sweater he wore for warmth were dirty and ragged.

He put the rubber stopper in the sink and turned on the water. Steam floated up and Johnny held his hands over it relishing the warmth. He dipped his hands into the warmth and then reached for one of the balls of soap. A drop of dirty water fell from his hands into the soap bowl as he struggled awkwardly to capture one of the dainty balls. His mind struggled with how he would remove the balls of soap in order to clean up the dirty water he had splashed on them. He rubbed a ball between his palms, and a soft scented lather appeared.

He washed and washed, but as he reached for a towel to dry his hands, a large dirt spot appeared on the white soft terry. He returned to the sink and scrubbed longer. When he could wipe his hands without leaving a dirt smudge on the towel, he considered it good enough. He tried to fold the towel so the smudges were hidden. He took a piece of tissue paper and tried to dab at the dirty water on the unused soap balls and their resting place. Tiny pieces of tissue stuck to each ball. He sighed in resignation and walked back into where his brother was lying.

"Do you think you can make it into the bathroom and wash up a little?" Johnny asked Joey. "Don't worry about making a mess, I've already accomplished that for us."

He helped his brother up off the bed and into the bathroom. He turned the towel back around to the smudged area. "Maybe you would want to wipe your hands on this side. Then we'll only have it to hide."

Johnny was glad that Joey was too short to see into the mirror. He shouldn't have to see what would stare back, not only the dirt, but also the sunken eyes.

Joey washed up. "What's on the little soap balls?" he asked.

"Never mind," Johnny replied.

With Joey settled back on the bed, Johnny still stood, not wanting to dirty the over-stuffed furniture decorating the room.

Charles and the cook entered the room carrying two trays. The one for Joey was hot, creamy chicken soup and warm biscuits and butter.

"This shouldn't be too hard on your throat," Charles said to Joey. To Johnny he gave turkey and dressing and cranberries with a tall glass of milk. Johnny could not remember the last time he had milk. He had made sure that if any came his way, he had given it to Joey.

"Wouldn't you like to sit down to eat?" Charles asked Johnny.

Johnny looked down at his pants and replied, "No, thank you. I'll stand."

Charles walked into the bathroom and brought out one of the towels and laid it over the cushions of the chair. "There. If that is what you are worried about, make yourself comfortable. It might as well look like the other one hanging in there." He smiled, and Johnny sat ever so carefully on the towel.

*****

Never had anything tasted so wonderful. Johnny ate until he felt as though he would burst. He hated the fact that he could not finish eating what was on his tray. Evidently, the many months of doing without had forced his stomach to become smaller. He finished off his glass of milk and carried the tray to the bathroom to set it on the counter.

Joey, however, did not fair as well. His throat was so sore that even to swallow the soup was hard, and to eat the biscuits was impossible. He sipped at his milk until Jesse and the doctor entered the room.

Johnny again took his place in the corner, not wanting to be in the way of either the doctor or Jesse.

The doctor prodded and thumped and tested Joey. Then, returning his eyeglasses to his pocket, announced, "It is good you got in touch with me. He is a very sick young man. What he has can be treated, but if it had gone untreated, his life might have been cut very short. What he has is a virus that could have resulted in rheumatic fever. With rheumatic fever, the heart can be damaged. However, with antibiotics and complete bed rest, he should be able to get back on his feet. He does, however, suffer from malnutrition, which will result in his recovery taking a much longer time. I will need to check on him periodically to make certain the antibiotics are working. Where will he be staying?"

Thoughts flew through Johnny's mind at the speed of light. Where would they be staying? He needed to find a place much warmer than the boxcar. He needed to be able to beg, borrow or steal food, if necessary, so Joey could get better. Desperation set in as he struggled to find answers to his questioning mind.

"He will be staying here," Jesse responded. "Both he and his brother will be here until he can get back on his feet again. Do whatever is necessary for him to regain full health. Don't worry about the expense. Just bill me for any costs incurred."

Johnny started to object, but urgency had replaced his pride. He needed help desperately.

He bowed his head and whispered, "Thank you, Sir."

The doctor slid his stethoscope back into his bag, and Jesse led him outside the room and shut the door.

"And what about you, Jesse? How are you feeling?" the doctor asked the gentleman now that the door was shut and they had gained privacy.

"I'm doing fine," Jesse answered. "I have some days that are better than others."

"Is having these two boys in your home going to make things more stressful on you?" He asked with concern, as he once again retrieved his stethoscope from his bag and placed the end on Jesse's chest to hear the strained thumping coming from inside.

"I'm sure I will be fine," Jesse answered. "I have staff to help take care of young Joey, and as for his brother, I am confident he will take care of himself."

"Where did you find a couple of young hobos to take into your home?" the doctor asked, once again returning the stethoscope to its place within his bag.

"They were sitting outside my window,"

Jesse answered. "They were searching for Christmas, and, for whatever reason, thought they could find it here."

"Where did they come from?"

"From some hobo jungle, I'm not sure where."

"There are so many of them around. It's a shame that something can't be done. It's for certain President Hoover isn't helping matters. Jesse, your heart is struggling. You need to get more rest and..." his voice faded not wanting to continue. "You should get your things in order."

"Thank you for coming Gerald," Jesse replied, helping the doctor on with his coat. "I will take your advice."

The doctor descended the winding staircase as Jesse buttoned his shirt. He knew how important it was for Joey to follow the doctor's orders, and he would see to it that Joey did. That little boy would not become as Jesse had become. He knew too well the effects of rheumatic fever. It was the same demon that now left his own heart struggling to beat. Jesse smiled to himself, remembering the little boy sitting in the snow beneath his window, defending his big brother with all his might. A large heart lived within that child, a heart full of love for his brother. It would not be damaged.

*****

Jesse re-entered the room. Johnny stood looking out the window, while Joey had drifted off into the wonderful world of sleeping in a warm bed.

"What are you thinking?" Jesse asked.

Johnny turned to Jesse. He was an older gentleman with gray hair neatly cut, with gray sideburns that came halfway down his cheek. His heavy brows sat above the steel blue eyes that looked as though he could see right through Johnny. When Jesse smiled, his eyes closed halfway, twinkling as the small lines created by smiles appeared at the corners. Johnny's father had had the same eyes. For a moment, Johnny felt as though he were looking into the eyes of his dad.

Jesse's smile was broad, and his teeth white and straight. When he spoke, there was a hint of a Scottish accent that Johnny remembered in his grandfather. It caused him, for an instant, to become homesick. His mind sprang back to reality. He had no home.

"I was thinking how very lucky we were to look for Christmas here tonight," Johnny said, and seeing that his brother was sleeping soundly, he continued. "I was planning on taking Joey to the orphanage tomorrow. I knew that he needed more help than I could give him, and I didn't know what else to do."

Jesse noticed Johnny's eyes fill with tears as he turned to face the kind gentleman.

"I can't begin to thank you for the help you have given us. I'm not certain how, but I promise, in someway, I will pay you back for your kindness."

"Where are you from, Johnny? Where did you live before you were forced out on your own?"

"We lived in a little town in southern Illinois," Johnny said. "It seems like a million miles from here and a lifetime away since we were there with our parents."

"What are your plans?" Jesse asked as he removed the towel and sat down on the chair that had been placed for Johnny. "I know the depression has affected many youngsters like yourselves, forcing many of you out of your homes. Have you thought about where you will go from here?"

"Earlier today I had decided to put Joey

in the orphanage, so he could get some help. I didn't know what I was going to do then. Now that Joey has been able to see the doctor, I will have to decide what we will do next. I will need to see to his needs until the Big Trouble ends and I can get a job. Somehow, someway, I am going to be a working man just like my father. He worked in the coal mines, just as his father did before him, and I will do the same. I want to do him proud. I want to have a home for Joey and me, and I want Joey to be able to go to school."

"That sounds like a lot of responsibility for one so young," Jesse replied.

"My grandfather immigrated to the United States from Scotland when he was not much older than I am. He came by himself. He had no one but himself. He had wanted to send back to Scotland for his parents and his brother, but he was never able to. If he could do that, then I can provide for Joey and me. The depression can't last much longer."

"What is your last name, Johnny?" Jesse asked.

"McCarvy," answered Johnny."

"McCarvy," Jesse responded. "What was your father's name?"

"William, Sir. Just like his father's."

A pensive look came over Jesse's face as he asked, "What about you going to school? Wouldn't you want that?"

"It's a waste of time to want something that you can't have. It burns up a lot of energy too, energy that I could be using to accomplish what I need to do. Besides, I can read. As long as I can read, I can learn."

"Do you like to read?" Jesse asked Johnny.

"I love to read. It seems like when I am reading, I can be anything I want to be, go anyplace I want to go. Money doesn't stop me. My age doesn't stop me. Not even the Depression can stop me. Of course, I can only read what I can find. Sometimes I find old newspapers or magazines. Someday, I will go to a library."

"Come with me, Johnny," Jesse said, opening the door. He led Johnny down the hall and through double doors leading into a large room. A fireplace crackled in the corner casting a warm glow across the wooden floors. Two high-backed chairs of green leather faced the fireplace. A mahogany desk shined to a luster sat in the center of the room. As Jesse turned on the lights, Johnny gazed in wonder at the shelves of books that surrounded the room.

Jesse smiled at the look of awe that came over Johnny's face. "Feel free to come and choose any book you like. It will help fill your time while your brother is recuperating," Jesse said.

"Thank you, sir," Johnny replied running a finger down the spine of a beautiful green leather book. Upon it, engraved in gold lettering, were the words "Gulliver's Travels."

"Sir?" Johnny said as Jesse turned to leave. "If there are any chores you would like done while I am here, I would appreciate the opportunity of doing them. I appreciate your generosity, but I really would feel better if I could work to earn some of it."

"Very well," Jesse replied. "In the morning ask the cook to introduce you to Edward, the grounds keeper. He will be able to line some work up for you to keep you busy."

"Thank you, sir," Johnny replied.

"Johnny?" continued Jesse. "Do you have any other clothes besides the ones you have on?"

"No, sir. I don't," Johnny replied, looking down at the rags he wore.

"Very well, then," Jesse replied and

walked from the room, leaving Johnny surrounded with a roomful of adventures.

Johnny walked around the room, examining row after row of books. He paused at the fireplace and felt the warm glow against his face. For the first time since his father and mother had died, he felt a sense of peace come over him.

"Johnny?" the voice came from behind him. "My name is Edward. I take care of the grounds of the manor. I was told you would be helping out and that I was to show you to your room."

Edward led him to his room. The servants' quarters were in the small house that sat behind the mansion; small in terms to those who owned a mansion. To others, it could be considered a mansion unto itself.

His cot, as Edward had called it, was a single bed with warm woolen blankets and a pillow of down. In the corner sat a pot-bellied stove, already warming the room. Johnny walked to the window that overlooked the stables and watched the snowflakes drifting softly to the ground. He looked towards the heavens and as the snowflakes did their never-ending dance, Johnny whispered, "Please God, bless the people of the jungle. Please help them."

He pulled the crisp sheets and warm blankets up under his chin. He marveled at how wonderful it felt to sleep warm. He thought of Joey, safe in the mansion, and once again looked to the heavens and said a silent prayer. "Thank you God."

Peace filled him as he drifted off to sleep.

*****

The next morning, Jesse was wakened by the sound of a shovel scraping the driveway. He looked out his window to see Johnny shoveling the long lane that he had carried his brother on. He wore the same clothes with the collar of his oversized coat turned up to his chin. Rags were wrapped around his shoes and around his hands to ward off the cold.

Jesse dressed and went down to breakfast, first checking in on young Joey.

"How are you feeling this morning?" Jesse asked.

"Better, Sir," Joey replied in a still faint voice. "I think I will be better by tomorrow."

"I wouldn't count on being better by tomorrow, young man," Jesse replied, smiling. You've been very sick, and it is going to take a while for you to get back on your feet. Don't become impatient."

"But we shouldn't take advantage of you," Joey answered. "You have been very kind to me and Johnny. We will be out of here as soon as we can. Maybe when I'm better, I can help do some chores to pay you back. Johnny wouldn't be here if it weren't for me."

"How did you two young men become so proud?" Jesse asked, sitting down in the plush chair beside Joey's bed. "You know, it is not a sin to accept help."

"Johnny said we should try and earn our way," Joey answered. "Our Pa always earned his way."

"Your parents did a fine job in raising you two young men," Jesse said. "Tell me about Johnny."

"He's my brother," Joey answered. "He's taken care of me, ever since our Pa and Ma died. He used to go to school, but that was before the Big Trouble came. He used to play baseball. He wanted to be a professional baseball player someday, but not anymore. Now he just wants to work and get a home for us. Someday, when I get a little older, I will be able to help. We are going to have a house and food and beds, and Johnny said that I could even have a dog. You don't think the Big Trouble will last forever, do you?" Joey asked Jesse.

"No," replied Jesse. "I don't think the Big Trouble will last forever. Someday it will be over, and people won't even realize what it was like."

"Good," Joey said. "Johnny said it's good not to remember bad things, that we should just learn from them."

"Your brother is a very wise person," Jesse replied, being interrupted by Emerson at the door.

"Your breakfast is ready, Uncle," Emerson's voice preceded him through the door. A look of disdain blanketed his face as he looked at Joey. "I hope you have someone watching the other hobo. He's probably stealing from you as we speak."

"Actually, Emerson, I have been keeping an eye on him. I saw him from my window shoveling the drive this morning. Perhaps you should be the one to watch him. You might learn from him."

Emerson huffed, turned on his heel and left with Jesse smiling behind him.

"Don't pay attention to Emerson," Jesse said to Joey. "All of us are born with our own set of problems. Emerson just doesn't realize that he is his own worst enemy. If there is anything you need, let us know," Jesse ruffled the hair on Joey's head and turned to leave.

"Sir?" Joey said. "Merry Christmas."

"Thank you, Joey, and a Merry Christmas to you also."

He followed Emerson toward the dining room for Christmas breakfast. Emeline, Emerson's mother was already seated at the table with several other guests.

For a moment Jesse's mind drifted through memories of his beloved wife. How she had loved Christmas. She started planning the holiday the day Thanksgiving ended. She had the spirit of a child when it came to the magic of the season. A child, he thought. She had wanted children of her own so badly, but it was not meant to be. He longed for her to be with him today, to walk arm in arm into the dining room and greet their guests, but he longed for her so many times for so many reasons. He would place the white and red poinsettias at her grave later today, as had been his tradition each Christmas day since her passing five years ago. He would kneel down beside her to whisper words of love. He would tell her to wait for him and that someday they would be together again. Until then, he would keep his memories locked up tightly in his heart, surrounded by the love he felt for her.

"Merry Christmas," he said to his guests, as he entered the dining room. Their words of greeting echoed back.

Sarah, the maid, entered carrying hot coffee and orange juice.

"Sarah," Jesse said. "Would you set another place at the table and have Edward go tell young Johnny to come in and have breakfast with us before he freezes shoveling the driveway?"

"Uncle! Surely you are not going to have a tramp sit with us for breakfast, are you? Have you seen how he looks? Have you smelled how he smells? Surely, he will make all of us lose our appetites."

"That might not be such a bad thing," Jesse replied. "It looks as though your appetite may have been a little too hearty lately as it is. Sarah, do as I say."

"Yes, Sir," Sarah replied, quickly leaving the room. In a short time, Johnny entered, unwrapping the rags from his hands.

"You wanted me, Sir?" he asked looking

toward Jesse, his face red from the cold.

"Yes, Johnny. Why don't you sit and have some breakfast? The snow will still be there when you are finished."

Johnny looked awkwardly down at his clothing, and Jesse, upon noticing his reluctance, continued, "Don't worry about your clothing. It is what it covers that makes the man. Please, come join us."

Johnny sat down at the place prepared for him next to Emerson. Emerson slid his chair as closely to his mother as he possibly could. Johnny looked across the table into the faces of the other guests, who seemed not to be bothered by his appearance. Straight across from him he looked into a pair of dark brown eyes that he had seen before, and they looked back—the same kind eyes he had seen, which belonged to the girl who had given him the hot bread and honey sandwiches just a few days before. She smiled at him. He ducked his head, suddenly all the more aware of his rags. Breakfast was served

*****

Joey gained a little strength with each passing day. He stayed confined to his bed but Charles saw to it that he was entertained with playing cards and checkers and such. He actually looked forward to his time spent with the little hobo.

Charles would tell him of London, the place of his birth. He even shared some childhood pranks that brought a smile to the little boy's face.

Joey would tell him of life in the jungle. He told him how to jump a train, where to look for food, and how to try and keep warm. He told him of Old Joe and how he took care of him when Johnny had to be away, how he shared his boxcar with them and how he too had been a butler in happier times.

Somehow, whenever Charles left the bedside of his little chum, he felt a better man for the time spent. He felt gratitude.

Edward had found chores enough to keep Johnny busy, and Johnny hoped they were real items that needed to be done, and not just token chores to make him feel needed.

He cleaned the stables and fed and curried the horses. He made certain the driveways and walkways were free of snow and ice. He cut and carried firewood for the eight fireplaces in the mansion. He fixed tires and replaced them and helped Edward paint the inside of the servants' quarters, where Emerson had made it very clear, he was to stay.

"If you must enter," Emerson had said, "use the servants' door in the back. We would not want our friends seeing a tramp entering the front door, and please, only enter when it is necessary."

"Thank you. I will," Johnny had said, still very aware of his place. Emerson could not have conceived how wonderful it was to enter through the servants' door. How wonderful it was just to feel warmth on your face as you entered, and to smell the aroma of bread baking in the kitchen, and to smell the clean scent of soap, as the kitchen was being cleaned and wax was being applied to the floor. But then, Emerson had not shivered so hard in the cold of night that his muscles ached. He had not gone for weeks without being able to bathe, nor had he rummaged in garbage cans looking for food, not to relish but just to sustain. He had not heard the cry of hungry children and the sobs of mothers not able to feed them. For Johnny to enter through the servants' door was a blessing and not an insult, but how could Emerson have known?

*****

Johnny had finished feeding the horses. The stalls had been cleaned twice that day. As he sat down on a bale of hay to fix a harness, Jesse entered through the barn door carrying a bag.

"Edward told me you would be here," he said. "It's dark outside. Don't you think it's quitting time?"

"I was about to quit, as soon as I fixed this," Johnny said, as Jesse sat down on a hay bale next to him.

"I'm a little curious," Jesse began. "What were your mother and father like?"

Johnny found it hard to believe that Jesse would show so much interested in a hobo boy.

"They were good people," he answered. "Ma was a wonderful cook. My dad would say she could take a sow's ear and make it taste like the finest ham. She would make what she called poor man's soup, but it tasted wonderful. She was always kind to everyone. I don't think she hurt anyone's feelings in her whole life. She was pretty. She didn't have make-up for her face or fancy clothes, but she was pretty. She always told my dad that he made her feel pretty no matter how she looked. She was God fearing and God loving. She always had so much faith, faith that everything happened for a reason and that if we just try to do what is right through the hardest circumstances, that someday we will see the purpose of all things and be stronger from it. Ma was a good mother." A lump formed in his throat and he swallowed hard to make it leave before tears had a chance to form in his eyes.

"What was your father like?" Jesse questioned.

"Pa was a good man. He believed in an honest day's work for an honest day's pay. He would never cheat anyone. His word was his law, and everyone knew it. He loved my Ma. I guess that if there is anything in the world that a pa can give his kids it is to love their ma. He loved her, and she loved him right back, and they loved us. They were good parents. I just hope Ma's right."

"Right about what?" Jesse asked.

"About there being a reason for all things. Right now, I can't see much reason for everything. Please, don't take me wrong. I don't mean our being here. I mean, well, our having to put you out like this."

"You're not putting anyone out," Jesse said looking around the barn. "As I see it, we are getting the best of the bargain."

"You've mentioned your grandfather coming from Scotland," Jesse continued. "What was he like? Did you know him well?"

"Not well enough." Johnny answered. "He worked in the coal mines, too. There was an explosion, and Grandpa was pinned under the timber. It crushed his chest and punctured one lung. He didn't live long after that happened, and Grandma had died before him.

"He used to sit me on his knee and tell me about Scotland and the Highlands. When he was buried, Dad laid his plaid in the casket with him. Grandpa had said his clan wouldn't let him into Heaven if he didn't have his plaid with him."

Jesse listened intently to Johnny, and at one point seemed to wipe a tear from his eye.

"When was the last time you went to a party?" Jesse asked Johnny.

"I think the only parties I went to were the ones we had at school sometimes, you know, like Valentines and Christmas and such."

"Would you like to come to a New Year's Eve party?" Jesse asked.

"A New Year's party?" questioned Johnny.

"We're having a New Year's Eve party tomorrow night. Why don't you come?"

Johnny looked down at his ragged

clothes. "I don't think your guests would be too impressed with your choice of people if I came," Johnny replied, "especially Emerson."

"Emerson is a bit of a snob, isn't he?" Jesse replied almost laughingly. "You know, Johnny, between the two of you, you are the richest."

"Oh yes," Johnny replied sarcastically, "and anyone would be able to tell that at a glance. It's my fine attire, and my debonair attitude, and of course, my fine education. Poor Emerson."

Jesse smiled as he continued, "Emerson's father was one of the richest men in town," he explained. "He had made his money in stocks and had quite the portfolio. When the market went down, so did the manner of living to which they had become accustomed. Shortly thereafter, Emerson's father died, leaving Emerson and my sister-in-law Emeline. As I said, they had become accustomed to a wealthy way of living, so I had them move in with me. You see, Johnny, with Emerson, the memories of his father are few. His father worked hard at the office and stayed late. He figured whatever job he had as a father could be accomplished with money. That is what he gave, and that is how he is remembered. The memories you have of your parents are wonder-

ful memories. Yours is the greatest inheritance."
Suddenly, Johnny was not so intimidated by
Emerson. He almost felt sorry for him. His mother's words came back to him. "The rich can be
poor."

"Here," Jesse said, handing the package
he had held under his arm to Johnny. "I thought
you might like something to wear to the party.
The package contained a suit with a silk shirt,
shoes and stockings and a tie. "Now you have no
excuse. We will see you tomorrow night."

"I hope Edward knows what to do with
this," Johnny said holding up the tie as Jesse
pushed back the large barn door and walked out
into the snowy night. Johnny followed, making
sure he used the servants' entrance to go up and
see Joey. "How are you doing, squirt?" he said, as
he peeked his head around the door.

"I'm feeling better," Joey replied, as he
put down the pencil and paper he had been
using. "What have you been doing today?"

"I've just been doing some chores that
needed done. I have something to show you,
though," Johnny said as he reached into the bag
and pulled out the clothes that Jesse had given
him. "Have you ever seen anything so nice?" he
asked Joey as he ran his fingers over the soft silk

shirt.

"Why did he give you those?" Joey asked, as he too ran his fingers over the fine cloth.

"He invited me to a party tomorrow night, a New Year's Eve party."

"Oh, Johnny. You're going to go, aren't you? Please go and then come up and tell me what it was like."

"I think I would feel out of place at such a fancy gathering, Joey, but he has been so kind to us that I feel if I refuse, it would offend him."

"Johnny?" Joey said and paused.

"Yeah, Squirt?" Johnny asked, as he put the clothes back into the bag.

"Johnny, there's something that I've wanted to tell you, but I haven't."

"What have you done?" Johnny asked, surprised by Joey's tone of voice.

"I haven't done anything wrong," Joey continued. "I just wanted to tell you something. I know you've had a hard time since Pa and Ma died. I know that I haven't made it easy on you, my getting sick and all. I just wanted to tell you thanks, and that, well...I love you."

"My gosh," Johnny said teasingly. "They

put you in a big fancy bed with all those frilly curtains and fluffy pillows and you go getting all soft on me." He rumpled the hair on his little brother's head. "You get some sleep, and I will come back tomorrow night and tell you what a fool I made of myself at the party. Deal?"

"Deal," Joey replied as Johnny walked out the door, turning before he closed it behind him.

"I love you, too, Squirt," he said as the door shut.

Back in his room, Johnny added a log to the fire. He brushed his hand once again against the fabric of the shirt, and gently put it back in the bag.

He gazed out his window to the frozen world waiting outside. Icicles hung from the roof and the snow glistened in the moonlight. Smoke from the chimneys drifted toward the sky, and again, he thought of those in the hobo jungle.

*****

Again the mansion was adorned. Festive balloons, confetti and streamers surrounded the ballroom. An orchestra performed the most fashionable songs of the present and the past, inviting the guests to join in. The banquet table was filled again. Champagne flowed freely. Fine guests in fine attire stood or mingled, as Johnny entered the room. Emerson was, as likely, the first to spot him.

"Uncle!" He said in alarm. "The tramp is here!"

Jesse turned to see Johnny at the door, dressed not in the suit and silk shirt but in his old clothes. They had been cleaned and ironed but still reflected the attire of the poor.

Jesse walked toward him to welcome him in and to question, "What happened to the clothes I bought you? Didn't they fit?"

"I'm sorry, sir, I didn't try them on."

"May I ask why not?" Jesse asked.

"They were fine clothes, and I do appreciate the offer, but they were mine weren't they?"

"Why, of course they were yours," Jesse answered.

"I took them back to the store and got the money for them instead."

"And why did you do that, Johnny?" Jesse asked.

"I could do without the clothes," Johnny continued, "but the food I bought because of them is something that the people at the jungle couldn't do without. I told them you were kind enough to send it down and they appreciated it so. It was the first time in months that some of the children had milk to drink. I hope you are not too disappointed in me. I didn't mean to offend you."

"No, I'm not one bit disappointed in you, nor have you offended me. I am disappointed in myself that I had not thought of that. Come on in, Johnny. Welcome."

"Uncle! Have you lost your mind? What are your friends going to think when they see you mingling with the likes of him? You have a reputation to think of, you know."

"Emerson, if they are my friends, they will not question my actions, and if they do, then perhaps they should not be attending," Jesse replied as he led Johnny by the elbow into the banquet room.

The dark-eyed girl walked timidly toward Johnny. "Haven't we met before?" she asked. "I don't mean at breakfast on Christmas day, but before then?"

"Yes," Johnny answered. "You were so kind as to give me bread and honey sandwiches one day not too long ago, and may I say that your kindness was enjoyed by more than a few people who were hungry."

"I'm glad it helped," she said blushing. "My name is Rachel."

They stood talking, and the night slipped by in what seemed an instant.

The hands of the clock slipped quietly toward midnight, and as the chimes started, balloons and confetti floated from the ceiling. Voices sang out "Auld Lang Syne," and "Happy New Year" echoed throughout the room.

There were none there that wished for a happy new year more than Johnny. He wished for himself and for Joey, but he also wished for all the others: those down trodden, those hungry and weary, those with hurting bodies and hurting souls, those who lived in boxes and those who lived in old car bodies, those who worried about tomorrow as they tried to survive today, those who had lost their dreams along with their dignity. He even wished for the poor rich, who needed to feel the richness of love. He wished for them all a happier new year.

Johnny carefully opened the door to Joey's room to tell him of the happenings of the night, only to find him sleeping soundly. He stoked the coals in the fire and tucked the covers up tightly around his little brother.

"Happy New Year, Joey," he whispered. "I promise I will make this year a better one for you."

He slipped quietly out of the room and found his way back to his sleeping quarters. He lay down in his cot and gratefully pulled the woolen blanket up around himself. The flicker of the stove shadowed the walls with dancing flames, as he drifted off to sleep to dream of the dark-eyed girl.

*****

New Year's Day blew in with a strong wind and heavy snow. Jesse again awoke to the shoveling of the driveway outside his window.

"I wish he weren't such an early riser," he said to himself. He dressed and had breakfast and again walked toward the barn.

"Good morning, Johnny," he said, shaking the snow from his coat as he entered the barn. "You were up bright and early this morning. I thought you might sleep in, since you spent most of the night talking to that lovely young woman."

"No, I couldn't sleep," Johnny answered. "Thank you for your understanding, sir, about the clothes."

"Ah, yes, the clothes. There is something I want to talk to you about. What are you doing today?"

"I was going to put some new lumber up in the tool shed," Johnny answered, "but if there is anything you would prefer I do...." he said, but was interrupted by Jesse.

"Would you like to go for a sleigh ride instead?"

"I have never been on a sleigh ride," Johnny answered. "I would like to."

"Get the sleigh hooked up to the mare and then pull it up front, and I will meet you there."

"You want me to drive the sleigh?" Johnny asked.

"There's nothing to it. Just flip the reins and say, 'get up,' to go and pull the reins and say, 'whoa,' to make her stop. I'm sure that a robust young man, who can drag himself up onto a moving train, can handle a sleigh. Meet me out front," Jesse said, as he turned and walked out of the barn.

After a considerable length of time, Johnny had the mare hooked up to the sleigh. He climbed up inside and with a flip of the wrist yelled, "get up." To his surprise, the mare took off. In front of the massive stone steps leading up to the mansion he yelled, "whoa," and pulled the reins; the mare stopped.

"That is easier than catching a freight train," he said to himself.

Jesse was waiting for him. He climbed up into the sleigh. Edward stood holding two quilts. He handed both up to Jesse to keep him and Johnny warm during their ride.

"Where are we going?" Johnny asked.

"To the jungle," replied Jesse.

Johnny looked puzzled.

"I want to see what the jungle is like," Jesse said. With the flip of the wrist, they were off, sleigh bells ringing as the sleigh darted across the snow. For the first time in years, the falling snow looked beautiful to Johnny. It would only last a moment until thoughts of the jungle would bring him back to the reality of what the cold can do to people.

As the sleigh entered the hobo jungle, people were huddled around the burning can trying to warm their hands. Others, who lived in the cardboard boxes and old car bodies, huddled together to ward off the cold. Smaller fires warmed scavenged garbage that would be their New Year's Day meal. All who had eaten the fine food that Johnny had brought the day before were still thankful for the kind offering from a man they didn't know.

The children of the camp, on hearing the sound of the sleigh bells, forgot the cold and ventured out to see who had come. As Jesse entered the jungle, his stomach ached at the sight of the poor unfortunate souls. The sound of babies crying and mothers weeping created pain in the faces of men who had no ways or means of trapping the demon causing their families to hurt. They would be angry, if anger helped, but it didn't; they would only be unavoidably hurt. The clothing they had was nothing more than rags. The silk shirt he had bought Johnny now seemed trivial and silly.

Johnny got down from the sleigh and said hello to Old Joe. He introduced Jesse to the fellow "Jungle-ites" as they called themselves. There was Artie, a slim young man with one leg. He had lost the other between two freight cars. There was Tex; a young man whose ears had frozen, and were now replaced by mounds of black flesh. There were girls in the jungle too; young girls who now resembled boys. Dresses had long since been replaced by baggie overalls and work boots, some with steel toes. Then there were the families, those who walked through the "Big Trouble" hand in hand, determined to make it together.

Jesse had heard of the hardships being faced by many Americans, but for the first time, he felt their pain. Something needed to be done. How could a country, as great as the United States of America, have its people living in huddled masses? "Huddled masses." His mind recalled the inscription on the Statue of Liberty.

"Give me your tired, your poor,

Your huddled masses yearning to breathe free,

The wretched refuse of your teeming shore.

Send these, the homeless, tempest-tost to me,

I lift my lamp beside the golden door."

*****

While Johnny visited with his friends, Jesse decided to take the children in the camp for a sleigh ride. He piled four or five children into the sleigh and covered them with the heavy quilts he had brought for Johnny and himself. Around and around the camp they went. Sleigh bells were ringing, and children's laughter was intermingled, with Jesse's own as it bellowed through the crisp winter air.

As Jesse lifted down the last of the children, he looked into the blue eyes of a small girl. Dark rings below her eyes were evidence that the little girl was not well. As he lifted her down, the cold winter air blew down her back and caused her to shiver. Jesse took the heavy quilt and wrapped it around her and handed her to her mother.

"Keep the quilt for her." He said.

The mother smiled back and with tears starting in her eyes, whispered, "Thank you, Sir."

The other quilt he handed to a young mother with a new baby huddled in her arms. She wrapped her infant in the quilt and whispered, "God bless you, Sir."

"No, God bless you," Jesse replied. "God, please bless America," he whispered, pleadingly.

The sun was setting as they pulled away from the hobo jungle. The impending cold of night sat hard upon Jesse's mind.

As they approached the mansion Jesse

said, "Take me out to the barn with you. I would like to talk, if you have time."

Once inside, Johnny started unhooking the mare from the sleigh.

"Tell me Johnny, if you had the money that I have, what would you do with it?"

"I don't think that will ever be a problem for me, Sir," Johnny answered.

"But, if it were, what would you do?"

"Well," Johnny said, "I would want to have a house, just a small one that would give Joey and me a home. Then I would like to have food for three meals a day, not fancy meals, just three home-cooked meals. Then I would like to save some to send Joey to school, so he could amount to something."

"And what about you? Wouldn't you want something for yourself?"

"I would still want to be a working man. Anything else I could want, I would get by working. A person doesn't need a lot in this life. I have seen people survive on what others throw away. I think the thing is to be grateful for what you have. A lot of people don't realize how nice it is to be warm, even though they are warm. They don't realize how good it is to eat when they are sitting at their own table. The cold, wet weather is just an inconvenience to them until they go under their roofs, and then they forget about it. I will never forget what it is like to be hungry or cold or homeless, so I guess it won't take a lot to make me happy in my life."

"So, if you had a modest home, food, and an education for Joey, that is what you would want, that, and to be a working man. Is that right?"

"Yes, I couldn't ask for more."

"Then, what would you do with the rest? There would be a lot more, you know."

"I would want to help others have the same thing," Johnny replied, as he backed the mare into the stall and placed oats in her pail.

"That's what I thought," Jesse replied.

"Sir, could I ask a question without sounding nosy?" Johnny asked.

"Of course you can."

"You said that Emerson's father lost all of his money when the market went down. Why didn't you lose yours?"

"I guess you might say it was a miracle," Jesse said. "Just a few weeks before, something told me to take all of my money out of the market and see that it was protected. My financial advisors thought I was crazy. It was just a very strong feeling that I had and couldn't explain. I would try and brush it away, only to have it come back several times a day. Finally, I conceded that if I was feeling that strongly about it, that something was telling me to do it, and it should be done quickly, so I did."

"That's good," Johnny replied as he closed the gate. "Do you mind if I go up and see Joey before I turn in?"

"Of course not. Come, I'll walk with you."

Charles was playing checkers with Joey. Joey was winning, and Charles was taking a ribbing for it. Joey was looking much better. A week with good food and a warm bed was working miracles, along with the antibiotics he was being given. Johnny was certain that not worrying about what they were going to eat or how they were going to stay warm helped in the recovery process. There was actually a sparkle back in Joey's eyes.

"Hey, kid, how are you feeling?" Johnny asked as he sat down in the large chair.

"He's feeling well enough to beat me," Charles replied as he closed the checkerboard and put it away. "Is there anything you would like to have before you go to bed?" Charles asked.

"No, thank you Charles," Joey replied.

"Very well. I will leave you with your brother then," Charles said as he left the room.

"What have you been doing all day?" Joey asked. "I will be glad to be up and doing stuff."

"That is a good sign, Joey. You must be feeling better." Johnny told Joey about his trip to the jungle with Jesse.

"Johnny, when we leave here are we going back to the jungle?" Joey asked.

"I think we will have to," Johnny said, "at least for a while, then who knows?" He continued trying to sound convincing. "We might hop a train and head to California. You know you can reach right up and pick an orange off a tree in California, or a lemon if you want. It is warm there, and I bet I can get a good job. Don't you worry, though. I'm going to take care of you. As long as we're together we are going to be fine."

*****

Jesse had gone into his library. He sat down in the large chair behind the desk and picked up his telephone.

"George," he said to the voice on the other end, "I want to see you tomorrow. Bring all the information you have on the warehouse down on the pier. I know that it's Sunday, but I need to see you first thing in the morning." He leaned back in his chair and reached into his vest pocket and brought out the chain with the half crest. He smiled.

George Paxton arrived shortly after breakfast. He followed Jesse into the den and they closed the large oak doors.

"What is the status of the warehouse?" Jesse asked.

"It is vacant. It is still in good condition. The plywood that was put over the windows has kept vandals from breaking them out. There is no water damage from frozen pipes, as we had them drained," George explained.

"What about heat? Does it have any heat?"

"No, the furnace went out, and we never had it replaced, since it wasn't in use. We figured as long as the pipes were drained, it wouldn't matter if there was no heat."

"Is it plumbed for heat?" Jesse asked.

"Yes, the pipes are all in for steam heat."

"So all that is needed to heat it is a new boiler?"

"Yes, the smallest furnace would suffice, if you just want to heat it enough to work in," George replied.

"No. We need a large boiler, one that will make people very comfortable. Get with the City Zoning tomorrow. I'm owed some favors down there and it's time to collect. Tell them that. They'll rush this through for me. Do whatever it takes, but have it rezoned for an apartment complex. I want heat in that warehouse before tomorrow night. I don't care what it takes or what it costs."

"I'll get right on it. I'm sure that I can find a dealer who will be more than happy to supply a boiler. I'll get the men together, and, with the Good Lord willing, we will meet your deadline."

"Oh, don't worry about it. The Good Lord is willing," Jesse replied, smiling as he slapped George on the back.

George left to see about his business, and again Jesse was on the phone. He didn't leave the den for several hours, but as he left, there was a definite smile on his face.

The trucks began arriving early Monday

morning. They backed up to the front of the warehouse where Jesse had assembled several people to oversee the unloading. The warehouse had already been cleaned and dusted. Boards, that had prevented windows from being broken, were removed.

The first truck brought beds and mattresses. The second truck brought blankets and pillows and comforters. The third truck brought several large tables and chairs to accommodate hungry families. The fourth brought dishes and silverware and pots and pans. The fifth brought six cooking stoves. Truck after truck arrived, each with an assortment of its own. Each was unloaded and the items placed in the designated places. The final truck arrived with food, enough food to feed a jungle of people, for after all, that was what was intended.

*****

Johnny was busy working in the tack room when Edward found him. He told Johnny that Jesse wanted to see him in the library. Johnny could not imagine what he was being called for. He took time to wash his hands and smooth back his hair, and walked toward the house.

"Don't forget to use the servants'

entrance," Emerson stated haughtily, as he passed Johnny on the way. "I hope you have my gelding fed and brushed. You need to make sure the chestnut mare is groomed and fed also. I might be taking Rachel out for a ride this afternoon.

"They've been done," Johnny answered, in passing.

As he stepped through the door of the servants' entrance, the scent of hot biscuits greeted him. There is nothing like the smell of hot bread, freshly baked, or sheets dried outside on the clothesline, he thought to himself.

He declined a hot biscuit, offered him by the cook, although the temptation to accept was strong. He needed to see what Jesse wanted.

"Come in," Jesse called as Johnny knocked on the closed library doors.

"Edward said you wanted me," Johnny replied, as he entered the library and stood almost at attention.

A gentleman sat in the chair across from Jesse, his back toward Johnny.

"I do," Jesse continued. "Sit down. So, you want to be a working man? Well, I have a job for you. I know that it is a job that you have never done before, but I have full confidence in your ability.

Bart, I would like you to meet Johnny," Jesse said, acknowledging the gentleman, sitting across from him.

Bart rose from his chair, and extended his hand toward Johnny.

"Bart is an architect. I have hired him to renovate a warehouse I have down on the pier. Have you ever done carpentry before, Johnny?"

"No, Sir," Johnny replied. "I once built a tree house in our back yard, but it fell down. I guess that doesn't say much for my carpentry skills."

"Well, Bart will have a contractor there to supervise you, but I want you to supervise the other men who will be helping you."

"I'm sorry, Sir, but I'm a little puzzled. Why would you want me to supervise? I know nothing about building and have never had any experience in supervising men. I'm sure there are others who are qualified to do what you are asking me to do?"

"The reason," Jesse continued, "is that the men I am going to hire might not trust anyone else."

"What men are these?" Johnny asked, still puzzled.

"The men from the jungle," Jesse replied. Jesse laughed at the puzzled look on Johnny's face.

"Never mind. Have you ever driven a truck before?"

"Yes, I worked on a farm one time and drove the farm truck," Johnny replied.

"Very good, then let's get going. Bart, meet us down at the warehouse at noon."

"Very well, Sir," Bart replied.

Jesse put on his coat and motioned for Johnny to follow him. Both of them climbed into the large panel truck waiting in front of the mansion. "Where are we going, sir?" Johnny asked.

"To the jungle, Johnny. To the jungle."

With three shifts of the gears the truck was off, headed to the hobo jungle. Johnny still did not understand.

*****

There were confused faces staring at the truck as it pulled in front of the boxcar that Johnny and Joey had called home. The large can still burned, creating the only warmth some felt.

All of the people gathered around upon Johnny's command, not knowing what was going on. "I'd like you to meet Jesse McCardy," Johnny said, nodding toward Jesse. "He's the one who provided the food for all of you on New Year's Day. I can assure you that although I do not understand completely what is going on, I do know that Jesse has a plan for the people of the jungle. It is a surprise. I can tell you this. I would trust this gentleman with my life, should I have to. So whatever he has planned, I am confident it will be in the best interest of all of us. He would like all of you to get in the truck. It may take two trips, so we will come back for those who don't take the first trip."

The people of the jungle were hesitant. Perhaps they should not have taken so kindly to the gentleman in the sleigh giving rides to the children. Perhaps he was going to take them to the jail where they would be separated from friends and loved ones. It was the little blue-eyed girl who first made the move. She walked up and held her hands up to Jesse. She was still wrapped in the quilt he had given her. He picked her up and kissed her on the cheek. Her mother followed, taking the child from Jesse's arms and stepped into the back of the truck. Her husband and others of the camp followed her. Soon the truck shifted and was off.

As the truck pulled up in front of the warehouse, the doors swung open. The scent of hot food escaped and drifted in the cold air straight toward the visitors in the truck. They stepped down and were guided through the open doors. Awaiting them was warmth, warm cots and hot food. The second load of passengers arrived to the same.

"Welcome to your new home," Jesse said when all were seated and eating. While you are here, you do not need to fear anything. All of your needs will be taken care of. There are however, two conditions. The first being that after you have taken a few days to rest, eat and gain strength, the men will be given a job. This warehouse is going to be converted into apartments. Each apartment will house a family. It will be the responsibility of the men to assist Johnny in the building of the apartments. It will be the responsibility of the women to see that these hard-working men are well fed. Food will be supplied. The second condition is this. Once a family finds work and is able to make it on their own again, they will give up their apartment to another in need. There will be no contracts to this fact. I do not fear that there will be any of you who will contest this. Now, eat up and have a good evening."

They were not ashamed of the tears of thanksgiving, these hobos of the jungle. Tears fell freely as they shook the hand of their kind benefactor and thanked him with full hearts.

"Johnny, would you drive me back, now?" Jesse asked when all of the guests were seated and enjoying the meal before them.

Back at the mansion, Johnny pulled the truck to a stop.

"Johnny," Jesse said. "When you have the truck parked, will you meet me in the library?"

"Of course, Sir," Johnny answered as Jesse stepped down from the truck. "What more could he possibly have to say." Johnny wondered.

The knock on the library door was answered with, "Come in Johnny."

Johnny entered to find Jesse sitting behind the large desk. He held in his hand a large opened Bible. He laid it down on his desk, and before he spoke, opened an envelope and removed a piece of paper and stared down at it for a moment.

"Do you believe in miracles, Johnny?

Jesse asked.

"I've never given them much thought," Johnny answered. "One doesn't see many miracles in the jungle, that was, until today. What you did was a miracle to all of us. Why do you ask?"

"My wife believed in miracles. She once told me that a hundred thousand miracles are happening every day and that most people are too blind to see them. I bet your mother believed in miracles, didn't she?" Before Johnny could answer that yes, his mother did believe in miracles, Jesse continued. "You came to my home on Christmas Eve in search of Christmas. Little did you know that in your search you would find me.

"Faith, Johnny, is a strange thing. It opens doors that a person doesn't even know exist. Your mother had such faith, and she instilled it in your heart, that faith that everything happens for a reason. I'm sure she didn't know at that time that a seed she was planting in your heart was leading you to me.

"You see Johnny. You and Joey were searching for Christmas, while I was searching for family. No," he paused, "it was more than searching for my family. I have been praying to find my family for a very long time.

"You see, I hired a private investigator

the day after you gave me this." Jesse reached into his vest pocket and pulled out the chain with the half crest attached. I received this letter from him today." He held up the envelope he had in his hands.

"Did your grandfather ever tell you about Ellis Island, Johnny?"

"No," Johnny answered, confused at where this conversation was leading. "I just know that he came to Ellis Island when he came to America."

"Let me explain something to you," Jesse continued. "At Ellis Island, there were many people who volunteered to help process the immigrants as they came into this country. They would ask the immigrants their names and do their best to write them down the way that they heard them. Sometimes, they were correct; sometimes they weren't. Sometimes, later down the road, if the immigrants' names were spelled incorrectly, they would have them corrected on their naturalization papers. Sometimes they just chose to keep the new name with their new country. That is what I chose to do. I kept my new name McCardy. My real name is McCarvy.

"Here, Johnny, this is yours," he said as he handed the chain and half crest to Johnny. He continued as he reached down and pulled an identical chain from around his neck, "and this is mine." He slid the two halves together to form a complete crest.

"Many years ago a young man left for America with the promise he would send for his father and mother and his young brother upon his arrival. After he left, his father died in a coal mine explosion. The landlord would not let his mother and brother stay on, if they could not produce, so they were forced into the streets to make it on their own. The young boy never again heard from his brother in America, that is, until now. Your grandfather, Johnny, was my brother. This is our family crest. We both came to America to find our fortunes. We both did. I found mine in money. He found his in you."

Johnny stood staring at the completed crest, unsure that his ears were hearing all correctly.

"Are you sure?" Johnny finally was able to ask.

"As I said, I hired a private investigator," he slid the letter toward Johnny. "He has all of the documentation necessary to prove that what he has written is true."

Jesse rose from his chair and walked

around the desk to Johnny. Embracing him, he whispered, "You and Joey are my brother's grandsons. You are my family." He looked into Johnny's eyes, and once more, Johnny recognized the eyes of his father.

"A hundred thousand miracles happen everyday, Johnny, and faith precedes each one. You thought it was your prayers that were being answered, but instead, it was mine."

I prayed to find my family, and you were sent to sit beneath my window searching for Christmas.

*****

Winter had been hard, but spring finally came and with it the resurrection of new hopes and dreams. The warmth of the summer brought with it new strength and vitality for Joey. He looked forward to starting school later in the fall. His health continued to improve. Jesse's did not.

The rain fell upon the casket, as each in attendance placed a rose upon it. Johnny had listened as tribute was paid to this man he had come to love so dearly. His heart ached with regret at not having known him longer, not having loved him longer. The tears blended with raindrops, as he now stood alone. He took an envelope from his pocket, whereupon his name was written. He opened it and unfolded the letter that had been tucked inside and read.

Dear Johnny:

I know that when you read this I will no longer be with you. I wanted to leave you knowing how incredibly fortunate I feel to have found you and Joey beneath my windowsill. I stand amazed that my prayers were answered so profoundly. What a gift I received that Christmas Eve!

We are all a part of an elaborate plan, designed and orchestrated by God. We each have a part to play and none of us knows how we will affect the lives of others as we play out our parts. When you traded your clothes to feed others, you started a wheel turning that would change the lives of countless of others, and courses of generations. We each have the opportunity to so influence the lives of others, if only we listen to our hearts. And so it is, by listening to my heart, I leave you in charge of my estate. Time will tell if our parts have been played well, for if so, God will smile. I rest in peace for your being in my life, and I know, that because of your being in my life, as you read this letter, God will smile on me.

With Love,

Jesse McCarvy

Johnny wiped away his tears, feeling not only his tremendous sense of loss, but also a tremendous sense of love. "Thank you," he whispered as he glanced toward the sunny sky. He took the white rose from his lapel and laid it on the casket.

"I love you, Uncle Jesse," he said so quietly that only the silence of the heavens could hear. "I will try always to do you proud."

Johnny looked down at the headstone shared by Jesse and his beloved wife, whereupon were inscribed the words:

"A hundred thousand miracles happen everyday."

He felt Rachel's hand slide into his. They turned and walked back toward the mansion.

Charles and his assistant butler stood holding open the massive oak doors. Old Joe, or Joseph, as he now preferred to be called, smiled as he asked, "Can I get you anything, Master Johnny?"

"No, Joseph." Johnny said, placing his

hand on his old friend's shoulder. "What could I possibly need?"

Joseph nodded, and smiled in agreement as he closed the door.

Epilogue

Johnny had been named executor of Jesse's will, in accordance with which he fulfilled the wishes of his uncle.

Emeline and Emerson were to be provided for, with the stipulation that each week, Emerson would donate a day's work to the homeless shelter, and each holiday season between Thanksgiving and Christmas, Emerson was to work in the soup kitchen of the local mission. He was also to use the servants' entrance.

The Christmas Search

"Johnny show me Christmas."
He heard his little brother say.
"Tonight is Christmas Eve,
And it's just a night away."
"Christmas is just another day.
Besides, you're very ill.
Just keep warm and get your strength,
And then next year I will."
"No, Johnny. Christmas just can't wait.
Let's go find it now.
If you'll just help me a little bit,
I'll have the strength somehow."
Johnny looked at the boxcar
That he and his brother both called home.
It was all two orphaned boys could have,
And not even theirs to own.
His brother was seeking Christmas.
Where on earth could it possibly be?
But this might be his one last wish.
So he would take him out to see.

"Come, get on my back," Johnny said,
"If that's what you want to do.
I'll carry you out to find Christmas,
If it's that important to you."
The mansion sat high on Manor Hill.
One could hear the music play.
The guests arrived in fine attire,
Pulled by a horse drawn sleigh.
The smell of roast goose and dressing
Sailed on the Christmas air.
If Christmas was to be found,
Surely they'd find it there.
His brother didn't feel heavy,
As he broke a path in the new fallen snow.
He could see the tree in the window.
They hadn't much farther to go.
Johnny lifted his brother down gently.
He spread his coat out on the ground.
"Sit here and peek through the window,"
he said.
"Be careful now; don't make a sound."
Mistletoe hung from each doorway.

Garland was laced down each stair.

The Christmas tree reached clear

to the ceiling.

The very grandest was there.

"Oh, Johnny, I'm glad we found Christmas.

It's everything I thought it would be.

I've often wondered what

Christmas was like.

Thank you for showing me."

"What are you two doing here?"

The voice behind them said.

"I don't recall inviting you.

Why aren't you home in bed?"

"Oh please, don't be mad at Johnny.

It's all my fault you see.

I asked him to help me find Christmas.

We came here because of me."

"What's wrong with you my child?

You don't look well at all.

Johnny, help me up with your brother.

Let's carry him into the hall."

As they lifted him up, his fevered brow

Brushed against the gentleman's head,

As he carried him up the staircase and

Laid him down in the down-filled bed.

"Johnny, go fetch the doctor.

Right by his side I'll stay.

Tell him to hurry as fast as he can.

Don't worry about the pay.

Your brother's going to get better.

You're so good to him and kind.

If it's Christmas that he's looking for,

Then it's Christmas he will find."

The years they came. The years they passed.

The two boys in the mansion stayed,

Blessed by the spirit of Christmas

They found on that special day.

Yes, Johnny and his brother found Christmas

And never from them did it part.

So if you happen to be searching for Christmas,

Don't forget to look in the heart.

By Susie Whiting

Taken from "To Christmas With Love"

Copyright 1995

Susie Whiting has written for family and friends over many years. She was encouraged by her children to publish her first book, "To Christmas with Love" in 1995. In 1998 she published her second, "A Message for Michael."

A Message for Michael

ISBN 1-55517-397-7 $4.95

Michael is a seriously ill little boy. Sarah needs a miracle to save her small son's life. Michael has been given a message to give to his mother, a message that will renew her faith in life and in love. He has a problem though—only he can see the messenger.

Based on a true story, "A Message for Michael" is a heartwarming story to read or to give.

To Christmas with Love

ISBN 0-9653276-0-4 $3.95

The perfect affordable gift, "To Christmas with Love" is a heartwarming collection of Christmas stories in poem form. "The Christmas Search" is one of the beautiful stories included.

Guaranteed to bring either tears, a lump in your throat, or goose bumps, "To Christmas with Love" is the perfect holiday book to read—a perfect gift to give.